D0442586

AFFAIRS

Other titles in this
series include:

AFFAIRS

Published in 2019 by The School of Life
70 Marchmont Street, London WC1N 1AB
Copyright © The School of Life 2019
Printed in Belgium by Graphius

A proportion of this book has appeared online at
www.theschooloflife.com/thebookoflife

Every effort has been made to contact the copyright holders of
the material reproduced in this book. If any have been inadvertently
overlooked, the publisher will be pleased to make restitution at the
earliest opportunity.

The School of Life is a resource for helping us understand ourselves, for
improving our relationships, our careers and our social lives – as well as
for helping us find calm and get more out of our
leisure hours.

We do this through creating films, workshops, books and gifts.
www.theschooloflife.com

ISBN 978-1-912891-05-4

Cover: Jean-Auguste-Dominique Ingres, *Paolo and Francesca*, c.1856–60

CONTENTS

A BRIEF HISTORY OF AFFAIRS

An affair is a romantic or sexual story between two people, one of whom (at least) is ostensibly committed to someone else. Most importantly, in our times, an affair is a catastrophe, pretty much the greatest betrayal that can befall us, a harbinger of untrammelled suffering, frequently the end of the marriage it has violated and almost always an occasion for fierce moralising and the division of participants into 'goodies' (those who have been betrayed) and 'monsters' (those who have betrayed).

However, in trying to understand affairs and make sense of their pains, as well as their less frequently confessed attractions, we should grasp that the way in which we interpret affairs today is very particular to our own times; we are remarkably contorted about the whole business, as judged against the long span of human experience. People have always had affairs, but what an affair means has been subject to huge changes across societies and eras. In order to gain a deeper picture of what we are doing when we look beyond our primary relationships, we need to glance backwards into the history – as well as briefly forwards into the future – of affairs.

Quito, modern-day Ecuador, 1532
The Inca sun-king Atahualpa owns private harems scattered across his empire; he is said to have had affairs with 3,000 women. Few subjects appear to think any less of him for this. All nobles have hundreds of

concubines. There are official regulations concerning the number of mistresses that anyone in government is allowed: a provincial governor can have up to twenty, the administrator of a small village, eight. Having affairs is no sinful slip; it is a central indicator of dignity and status.

Versailles, France, June 1745

The 35-year-old French king Louis XV has been married for twenty years, since the age of 15, to Marie Leszczyńska, daughter of Stanisław I, the deposed King of Poland, a woman whom no one expected him to love – and whom he duly doesn't. Now, Louis has developed a passion for the beautiful and gracious 25-year-old Madame de Pompadour, who is herself married. She quickly becomes the most prominent in a long list of Louis's lovers. The court is delighted for Louis and no one feels especially sorry for the queen, who devotes herself to music and reading and in time takes a few lovers of her own. A royal marriage is understood in terms of political and dynastic considerations, just as at other levels of society it is seen in terms of property or business interests: a way of uniting two pieces of land or of bringing a useful son-in-law into the family workshop. To marry for love is judged an entirely irresponsible eccentricity as well as a wasted strategic opportunity. The idea that a person should spontaneously want to have sex with their spouse once children have been conceived is deemed bizarre and – in essence – perverted.

Leipzig, Germany, April 1774
Johann Wolfgang von Goethe publishes *The Sorrows of Young Werther*, which becomes the most popular novel in Europe for the next thirty years. It is the pre-eminent expression of certain new Romantic ideas around

marriage: that we should only marry for love and that to sleep with someone outside of marriage is a grave offence, emotionally rather than religiously or socially. Nevertheless, the novel acknowledges that it can be deeply tempting to have an affair and that desire doesn't neatly follow legal rules. The hero of the novel has a flirtation with a married woman, but, because he cannot go further with her and is overwhelmed by his own longing, he ends up seeing no other option but to kill himself. The novel emphasises that an affair or even the prospect of one can be both a source of extraordinary delight and the harbinger of calamity. The stakes feel a lot higher now that marriage is meant to be so much more than a practical alliance.

Paris, France, 7th February 1857
The French writer Gustave Flaubert is narrowly acquitted of obscenity charges brought against his novel

Madame Bovary, the first detailed fictional description of sexual infidelity. The heroine of the novel, Emma Bovary, is driven to have an affair for a reason which her society now thoroughly condemns (though it would have been wholly unsurprising to Louis XV): she no longer sexually desires her husband, Charles.

We are firmly in the era of Romantic marriage, and affairs have become appalling phenomena because of the expectation that marriages should be lifetime unions based on enduring love and continuous sexual enthusiasm. By insisting that a marriage partner should be everything to their spouse (co-parent, domestic manager, erotic companion and soulmate), Romanticism turns an affair from a problem into a tragedy. Infidelity becomes the core theme of all the great novels of the second half of the 19th century. From *Anna Karenina* to *Middlemarch*, heroes and heroines have to die or grievously compromise their social positions following any forays outside of their vows.

Miami, United States, Sunday 3rd May 1987
The *Miami Herald* runs a story revealing that the married Democratic presidential candidate Gary Hart has been having an affair with Donna Rice, a sales representative for a pharmaceuticals company. Up to this point, Hart has been the front runner in the presidential race, but his campaign is upended by the revelation of his affair and after a week of meek protestations and contrite apologies, he withdraws. The leadership of the world's most powerful country has largely been decided on the issue of infidelity. An affair is not simply a private matter – it has become one of the sternest tests of a person's moral worth.

World Wide Web, May 1992

The Usenet newsgroup alt.polyamory is created and polyamory is formally defined for the first time as 'the practice, state or ability of having more than one sexual loving relationship at the same time, with the full knowledge and consent of all partners involved.' Polyamory suggests a remarkable break with the uncomfortable tensions of the Romantic theory of marriage. Rather than having to love only one person and then lie about any subsequent desires, one can – as a polyamorist – be transparent and enjoy multiple sources of affection. The whole idea of 'an affair' promises to disappear in a new wave of psychological openness. However, a central objection to polyamory is soon raised: that it has, with naive utopianism, entirely forgotten about the primordial power of jealousy.

Toronto, Canada, July 2015

The world's largest extramarital affair dating site, Ashley Madison, is hacked and 25 gigabytes of customer data is stolen. The hack provides the media with an occasion to consider the prevalence of affairs, and the response is one of predictable outrage. Analysis of users of the site reveals the line of reasoning behind why affairs appeal. Firstly, people love their spouses and are properly committed to their relationships. Secondly, they cannot help but be drawn to other people out of a mixture of boredom, passion and desire (the slogan of Ashley Madison is: 'Life is short. Have an affair.'). Thirdly, they know well enough that their partners could not take this on board without fury and immense hurt and therefore have to be deceived (unlike what polyamorists would hope for). For millions around the world, the dilemma is clear: We both desperately want to be married and equally badly need to experience sexual intensity with new people; neither complete fidelity nor singledom quite work. In the wake of the data hack, the consequences of this secret tension become especially acute: on 24th August 2015, a pastor and professor at the New Orleans Baptist Theological Seminary commits suicide after being exposed as a user of the site.

It becomes evident that under the aegis of Romanticism, humans have, collectively, evolved a very lovely but also very demanding set of thoughts: the view that a relationship should be founded on love, but also that having an affair must be a direct denial of this love – and therefore one of the worst and most hurtful things a person can do. At the same time, quite a lot of otherwise admirable people keep having affairs, or at least very much wanting to. Humankind is at an extremely difficult impasse. What, then, of the future of affairs?

Hellas Basin, Mars, 2150

Humanity, which has now colonised other planets, has moved to a new stance on affairs. An implant into the left temporal lobe of the brain has removed any tendencies towards feelings of sexual exclusiveness and jealousy. It is now, thanks to neurosurgery, possible to contemplate our partner having a little sex and some intimacy with another person without being totally destroyed by the notion. It has finally become possible actually to believe the phrase 'It didn't mean much'.

Like Romantics, people still get married for love, enjoying the continuity and deep intimacy the tradition allows; and at the same time, like Louis XV of France or the Inca king Atahualpa, they can enjoy affairs without tragedy. From their condominiums on the red planet, humans look back with pity at the risks that used to accompany straying lovers in the Romantic age, as well as shuddering at the mercenary coldness of marriages in the era before people got betrothed because they genuinely cared for one another. They feel, quite rightly, that they have evolved something far more complex and humane.

But for now we remain, in our earth-bound state, a long way off from such a frictionless utopia, and with plenty still to be tortured by.

WHEN DOES AN AFFAIR BEGIN?

Once an affair has been uncovered, we often ask – in the position of the betrayed, pained party – when it began. Pinpointing the precise moment promises to shed light on its motivations and on possible ways to prevent any further such disasters in the future.

There is, understandably, a hunt for the exact time when the two straying individuals met and physical contact began. We think of how two people had a drink after a business dinner, or met online, or flirted at a party and agreed to meet up a few days later. We concentrate on exact details: when their knees touched under the table, when one of them lightly put their arm round the other's waist and when they first lied about where they were going or to whom they were sending a message.

This kind of detective work feels obvious, but it overlooks a complexity: The start of an affair should not be equated with the moment when two straying people meet. *Affairs begin long before there is anyone to have an affair with.* Their origins lie with certain, initially minute fissures that open up within a subtly fracturing couple. The affair predates, possibly by many years, the arrival of any actual lover.

There is a somewhat parallel intellectual issue to which historians are trained to be alert. It is common to ask when a cataclysmic event like, for example, the French Revolution began. A traditional response is to point to the summer of 1789, when some of the deputies at the Estates General took an oath to remain in session until a constitution had been agreed upon, or to a few days later when a group of Parisians attacked and broke into the Bastille prison. But a more sophisticated and instructive approach locates the beginning significantly earlier: with the bad harvests of the previous ten years, with the loss of royal prestige following military defeats in North America in the 1760s or with the rise of a new philosophy in the middle of the century that stressed the idea of citizens' rights. At the time, these incidents didn't seem particularly decisive; they didn't immediately lead to major social change or reveal their solemn nature, but they slowly yet powerfully put the country on course for the upheavals of 1789. They moved the country into a revolution-ready state.

Likewise, affairs begin long before the meeting at the conference or the whispered confidences at the party. It is not key to fixate on the trip to Miami or the login details of the website. The whole notion of who is to blame and for what starts to look immensely more complicated and less clear cut. We should be focusing on certain conversations that didn't go well in the kitchen three summers ago or on the sulk in the taxi home five years before. The drama began long before anything dramatic unfolded.

This is how some of the minute but real causes might be laid out by a partner who eventually strayed:

Unending busyness

It was a Sunday morning, our beloved's time had been taken up for months on a big project and we'd been very understanding. Now it was over and we were looking forward to some closeness and a trip to a café. But there was suddenly something new that they needed to look at on their phone. We glanced over at their face, lit up by the glow of the screen; their eyes looked cold, determined and resolutely elsewhere. Or else they hatched a sudden firm plan to reorganise the kitchen cupboards just when we might, at last, have had a quiet time in the park together. That's perhaps when the afternoon of passion in Paris really began: with the need to stop everything in order to swap around the crockery and the glasses.

Neglect

We were away on an exhausting trip and in a break between meetings we fought for the chance to call them. They picked up, but the television continued on in the background; they had even forgotten we'd had to give a speech and it felt a little humiliating to have to remind them and to hear their lacklustre 'great' in response.

Shaming

We were with some new friends, people we didn't know too well, and we wanted to create a good impression. Our partner was looking to amuse them and, having cast around for options, opted to tell everyone a story about how we once showed the wrong slides in a presentation at work. They know how to tell a good story and there was a lot of laughter.

Ownership

Without discussing it, our partner arranged that we'd

both go and have lunch with their parents. It wasn't so much that we minded going; it was the fact that they didn't feel the need to ask us if we minded and if the timing was convenient. On another occasion, without even mentioning it, they bought a new kettle and got rid of the old one; it was as if we had no say at all. Sometimes they'd just tell us what to do – 'take the bins out,' 'pick up some dinner from the supermarket,' 'put on different shoes' – without adding 'please' or 'would you mind' or 'it would be lovely if ...'. Just a few words would have made a very significant difference.

Flirting

We were at a party with them and we saw them from across the room in deep conversation with another person. They were bending towards this person, saying something; they were laughing charmingly; they put their hand on the back of the other person's chair. Later they said it had been a very boring conversation.

One too many arguments

It wasn't the basic fact of having disagreements; it was the sheer number of them and their unending, repetitive nature. One that sticks in the memory was when we were at the seaside and things should have been happy for once – and yet they chose once again to ramp up the tension about a Thai takeaway that had been ordered. We remember arguing and, at the same time, one part of our mind disassociating, looking down upon the two of us standing on the pier with cross faces and wondering, 'Why?'

Lack of tenderness

We were walking in the street together near the market and we reached out to hold their hand, but they failed to notice. Another time, they were doing something at the kitchen table and we put an arm round their shoulder, but they said sharply, 'Not now.' In bed we're always the one to turn towards them and kiss them goodnight; they respond, but they never, ever initiate. This rankles more than it seems normal or possible to say.

Erotic disengagement

There was a sexual idea we'd been getting interested in, but we felt awkward about mentioning it to them. We tried to give a few hints, but they didn't give out the impression that they were curious; they didn't encourage us to expand. They gave us the sense that it would be a lot more convenient if we just kept whatever it was that tickled us to ourselves.

~

Individually, none of these things may be very dramatic. Some little version of one or another of them may be happening pretty much every day. And it's not all one-way: both parties are probably doing some of these things quite regularly, without particularly noticing or meaning to.

Yet a careful historian of infidelity might pinpoint any one of these as a moment at which – in a true sense – an affair began. Long before the party or the conference, the feeling was implanted deep in someone's mind (perhaps beyond the range of their conscious awareness) that there was something important missing in their relationship that another person might, perhaps, be able to supply.

It is common, when an affair is discovered, to become an inquisitorial prosecutor: to seize a phone and ask the 'cheat' in detail where they have been; to read through their emails and parse every receipt. But such assiduousness is a little late, a little misdirected and rather too self-serving. We should look further back than the moment when a lover came on the scene. The revolution didn't begin with the sexual act or the dirty texts – the actual storming of our domestic citadel. It began on a sunny, innocent afternoon many years before, when there was still a lot of goodwill, when a hand was proffered and when the partner was perhaps fatefully careless about how they received it. That might be a rather more painful account of our relationship and its troubles than either of us is ready to contemplate for now, but it may also be a more accurate and ultimately more useful one.

HOW TO SPOT A COUPLE THAT
MIGHT BE HEADED FOR AN AFFAIR

Having arguments does not, in itself, say very much about the likelihood of a relationship disintegrating. What matters is how arguments are interpreted, conducted and resolved. The fragile unions aren't necessarily the ones in which people shout, insist that this is finally it, call the other a ninny and slam the door; they are the ones in which emotional disconnection and rupture are not correctly identified, examined and repaired.

A number of qualities are required to ensure that a

couple knows how to argue well. There is, first and foremost, the need for each party to be able to pinpoint sources of discomfort in themselves early and accurately: to know how to recognise what they are unhappy about and what they need in order to flourish in the couple. This is not necessarily as obvious as we might imagine. It can take time and psychological insight to know that it was actually the missing phone call or the request to move the date of the holiday that is really the source of anger.

Then there is the equally vital quality of feeling that we have the right to speak, that we aren't duty bound to be 'good' and not cause trouble, that it is acceptable to say when we are miserable and when something – however small it might appear – is troubling us, that it is better to spoil a few evenings than ruin a marriage.

It can help to have a sanguine assessment of how human relationships tend to go: to accept that a bit of disappointment and some friction belong to the necessary ingredients of good-enough love, and that it isn't a disaster to be cross at points and seemingly convinced that this should be the end.

A subsidiary talent is the skill of knowing how to speak up. Diplomatic skills matter. It might not be exactly the moment the problem appears – we might need to wait until some of the surface tension has dissipated; perhaps the next morning can do just as well. We need to have a background confidence not to blurt out every objection in a panicked diatribe or shout a wounded feeling across the room when the other is themselves too upset to hear it. We need to know how to formulate our complaints into a convincing, perhaps even comedically framed point that has a chance of winning over its target.

It matters in all this that we both feel attached to the partner and, at the same time, have an active impression that we could walk away from them were matters ever truly to escalate. Feeling that we have options means that we do not, therefore, have to cling on. Feeling that we deserve good treatment ensures that our voice can be measured and that the status quo will remain manageable.

None of these factors tend to be present in those unfortunate couples who do not just argue but lack the gift of arguing well. A range of inner obstacles prevents them from dealing effectively with their emotional disconnection and anger:

Over-optimism about relationships

Fragile couples, paradoxically, tend to be very hopeful

about love. They associate happiness with conflict-free unions. They do not expect, once they have found the person they unwisely see as 'the one', ever to need to squabble, storm out of a room or feel unhappy for the afternoon again. When trouble emerges, as it inevitably does, they do not greet it as a sign that love is progressing as it should, but rather as alarming evidence that their relationship may be illegitimate and fundamentally flawed. Their hopes tire them for the patient tasks of diplomatic negotiation and routine maintenance.

Out of touch with pain

Fragile couples tend not to be good detectives of their own sufferings. They may be both unhappy and yet unsure as to the actual causes of their dissatisfactions; they know that something is wrong in their union, but they can't easily trace the catalysts. They can't zero in on how it was the lack of trust in them around money that rankles, or that it has been their behaviour towards a demanding youngest child that has been hurting. They lash out in vague or inaccurate directions, their attacks either unfairly general or unconvincingly specific.

Shame

A shamed person has fundamental doubts about their right to exist. Somewhere in the past, they have been imbued with an impression that they do not matter very much, that their feelings should be ignored, that their happiness is not a priority, that their words do not count. Once they are in a couple, shamed people hurt like anyone else, but their capacity to turn their hurt into something another person can understand, and be touched by, is recklessly weak. Shamed people will sulk rather than speak, hide rather than divulge, feel secretly wretched rather than candidly complain. It is frequently very late – far too late – by the time shamed people finally let their lover know more about the nature of their desperation.

Excessive anxiety

Complaining well requires an impression that not everything depends on the complaint being heard perfectly. Were the lesson to go wrong, were our partner to prove intransigent, we could survive and take our love elsewhere. Not everything is at stake in an argument. One of us hasn't ruined the other's life. We therefore don't need to scream, hector, insist or nag. We can deliver a complaint with some of the nonchalance of a calm teacher who wants an audience to learn but can bear it if they don't; we could always say what we have on our mind tomorrow, or the next day.

Excessive pride

It takes an inner dignity not to mind too much about having to level complaints about things that could sound laughably 'small' or that leave one open to being described as petty or needy. With too much pride and fear, it can become unbearable for a person to admit that they have been upset since lunch because their partner didn't take their hand on a walk, or that they wish so much that their partner would be readier to hug them last thing at night. We have to feel quite grown up inside not to be offended by our own more child-like appetites for reassurance and comfort. It is an achievement to know how to be strong about one's vulnerability. One may have said, rather too many times, from behind a slammed door, in a defensive tone, 'No, nothing is wrong whatsoever. Go away,' while secretly longing to be comforted and understood like a weepy, upset child.

Hopelessness about dialogue

Fragile couples often come together with few positive childhood memories of conversations working out; early role models may simply have screamed at and then despaired of one another. Fragile couples may never have witnessed disagreements eventually morphing into mutual understanding and sympathy. They would deeply love to be understood, but they can bring precious few resources to the task of making themselves so.

~

None of these factors mean there will have to be an affair, but they are generators of the states of emotional disconnection that contribute to an all-important affair-ready state. Outwardly, things may seemingly be well. A couple may have an interesting social life, some lovely children, a new apartment. But a more judicious analysis will reveal an unexpected degree of risk: An affair won't – in the circumstances, whatever it may later seem – be just an idle self-indulgence or a momentary lack of self-control. It will be the result of identifiable long-term resentments that a couple, otherwise blessed and committed, lacked the inner resources and courage to investigate.

THE ROLE OF SEX IN AFFAIRS

When an affair is discovered, it is common to describe the person who strayed as despicably sexually uncontained. They are lustful, wanton, dog-like. They have ceded control to their animal selves. But we can get a more nuanced view of the role of sex in affairs by asking a deliberately obtuse, philosophical-sounding question: Why is sex so nice?

One possible answer, which can sound a little odd, is: *because we have advanced tendencies to hate ourselves and find ourselves unacceptable* – feelings which sex with a new person has an exceptional capacity to reduce.

A long-term relationship can only too easily enforce a sense that we are neither very admirable nor very worthy. Management of family life, cleaning rotas, finances and relations with friends and in-laws can contribute to an impression that one is fundamentally troublesome and undeserving of sustained notice. The mood around us is fractious and ungrateful. 'Not you again' may be the implicit message one receives upon entering any room.

Physically, we have strict instructions to keep ourselves to ourselves. There is one person on the planet we are meant to be naked in front of, and this figure is unlikely to be particularly impressed or even vaguely cognisant of our appearance. With everyone else, we are cautious, swaddled beings. We would not dare to come within thirty centimetres of most of humanity.

And then, suddenly, in the context of an affair, everything changes. We can be enlaced and carefree. Our tongue, normally carefully shielded and used only to form sounds and break down toast or our morning cereal, is given permission to enter another person's mouth. We are no longer just the person who makes problems with the in-laws and doesn't lift their weight around the house or with the finances; we are someone whose very essence has, via the flesh, been witnessed and endorsed.

What we may be doing is slipping off another's top or inviting them to release our trousers, but what all this means is that another human has – exceptionally – chosen to find us worthy.

For so-called cheats (who will most likely have to pay a very heavy price indeed for going to bed with another person), sex can have remarkably little to do with 'sex'. It is an activity continuous with a range of non-physical needs for tenderness, acceptance, care and companionship. It is an attempt – negotiated through the body, but focused on the satisfactions of the psyche – to make up for a long-standing, painfully severed emotional connection with a primary partner.

THE ESSENCE OF WHAT WE
FEEL UPSET ABOUT

A s betrayed parties, we fixate – understandably – on what happened physically. We replay again and again the thought of what our partner did with their new companion. It seems horrific that they should have let lust control them in this way.

But to try to understand the true source of our devastation, we might distinguish between two kinds of things they have done. We may not necessarily know many details, but the thoughts and images that flit through our minds can be broadly divided into two kinds as shown in the table overleaf:

A: Bodily things they did	B: Emotional things they did
They took their clothes off urgently	They looked into each other's eyes and smiled
They had sex for two hours in a hotel	They made up nicknames for each other
They sucked each other's fingers	They talked of their sorrows and cried with one another
They watched each other masturbate	They shared moments of giddy, child-like joy

Typically an affair is defined by the ingredients in column A. But the things that truly upset us may be the elements of emotional engagement, as we imagine them, in column B. It may not, strictly speaking, be the idea of our partner (for instance) taking their clothes off in front of another person that is at the heart of our pain; it's the way we imagine them thinking and feeling; it's the nicknames they might have made up for one another ...

This tells us something important. The crucial, active element in an affair isn't really the physical sex per se: it's the connection, the intimacy, the sense of closeness, the warmth, the shared liking for which physical sex provides the occasion.

The thought opens us up to a more defined, perhaps more searing and yet, usefully, more accurate avenue of pain in relation to our partner. The problem is not that they have been horny – something for which we cannot really be held responsible and which we can therefore safely moralise about. It is that they have been lonely – something which it is a great deal harder to bear and think ourselves wholly innocent of.

THE PLEASURES OF AFFAIRS

Given the pain infidelity may cause, it can feel callous to explore the charms and attractions of affairs; it's a move that our Romantic age can be extremely censorious about. But it is difficult to make any sense of our escapades unless we can first understand what may be so powerfully compelling about them. We cannot secure the understanding of relationships that we need so long as we remain willingly blind to the more thrilling facets of 'straying'.

There are several important ways in which an affair can feel urgent and important, despite all the complications and dramas it may embroil us in:

Foregrounding neglected parts of who we are

A central peril of long-term relationships is their corruption of our sense of identity, their habit of caricaturing us in unhelpful directions. At home, over the years, we become simply 'the bossy one', 'the intellectual one', 'the organiser', 'the lazy one' or 'the one who frets stupidly about money'. The description may not be wholly untrue, but it is – crucially – woefully limited.

However, with our lover, we have the chance to start the story of ourselves anew. Whatever we may feel about them, it is how they make us feel about ourselves that can be at the core of their appeal. In their company, we can present facets of who we are that have been sidelined in our main relationship. We can discover a more carefree side of ourselves, or emerge as the one who takes the lead in making decisions. We are not boxed in by assumptions that might have been mostly true a decade before. The lover declares us to be, much to our surprise, but also to our relief, remarkably funny, relaxed or serious – things we might have struggled to feel in the face of the prejudices of our partners, who tell us with authority what we are 'really' like.

In long-term love, we are the prisoners of history. Nothing has been forgotten: the weekend city break when we shouted, the Christmas when we forgot the present, the anxious period after the sacking when we ruined a whole summer. We don't wish to lie about who we are; we want a chance to be properly forgiven, which may mean in practical terms that someone should simply not know the whole of our story.

Kindness

One of the great perils of an established relationship is that it cuts us off from our longing to be kind. We are so often left fighting for our basic rights within the couple that we have no opportunity to give expression to our appetite for generosity and sweetness. We have to persuade our partner to let us have an allotted amount of time to ourselves. We have to point out that we have already compromised on a given issue. We have to put our foot down about certain domestic chores. We have to remind our partner on many occasions to do something they had solemnly agreed to do but are reneging on. We have to take issue with a cutting comment levelled in our direction. For much of the time, it feels as if we might be fighting for our lives.

We can grow very resentful. Our capacity to be kind becomes hampered by our memory of the other's unkindness to us. We would like to prepare them breakfast and surprise them with a present, but we can't forget the way they mocked us at the party or were ungrateful about the help we gave their sibling.

Yet within an affair, we can throw off the watchful and suspicious stance we have adopted. The delight isn't just that the lover is nice to us; it is that we can be so nice to them, the way we always longed to be and knew we were when we first began to dream of love in adolescence. They have not hurt us (yet), nor given us grounds for vigilance. In the hotel room, we can give untrammelled expression to a passionate wish to be helpful, to listen, to be generous, to do little things to make them comfortable, to be attentive to their needs, to show them special signs of respect and to pay them compliments. We are reminded that being emotionally stingy was only ever a response to upset.

The simplicity of the task

We are normally trying to be so much: a co-parent, a domestic manager, a sexual companion, a friend. Unsurprisingly, we fail at most of these tasks. But affairs are mercifully simple propositions. We are not trying to do laundry and fathom someone's intimate history. We are not juggling a homework schedule and attempting a sexual scenario. We don't have to manage their mother and their soul. We have a rare chance to do one thing well.

Our faith in human nature is renewed

We learn, in established love, to be cautious in our hopes for what another human can be like. We know that people don't generally change very much. We grow to accept that most attempts to persuade our companions of anything will fail. We accept how much intransigence we will meet with. We understand that luck seldom comes our way.

But an affair is a rare break. Despite everything we have become, another member of our species has opted to give us a chance. They have looked at us with new eyes and, for once, not found us wanting. They have chosen to glance past our flaws and it is as if we are reborn through their original, creative gaze.

We regain a little faith in the whole human project. We

receive an uplift which spreads across all areas of life. One very special person gives us energy to look anew at the whole species. For the first time in many years, we smile benignly and open-heartedly at existence.

An end to shame

We grow used to being burdened by a sense that a lot of what we are deep down is unacceptable. Sex becomes the fulcrum of the censorship. The other doesn't want to know our more intimate fantasies. They roll their eyes when we describe a passing daydream we had about a colleague or someone on a train. We are acutely aware of how disgusting some of what we want can feel to them after an exhausting day with the children. But no such taboos are in place with a new love. They welcome our extreme sides as evidence of trust and intimacy. They, too, long to do things that respectable people might shudder at. Our union is a conspiracy against judgement. We do so-called disgusting things as a way of proving our degree of inner purity and commitment.

The world is bigger than we'd thought

The world has, without our really noticing it, grown predictable and stale. Our expectations are fixed. Our knowledge seems established. But the lover is showing us that life is so much richer than we had dared to think. The vastness of the cosmos comes through in little details. They have a completely different idea of what a bathroom or a kitchen can be like. They read an alternative newspaper and have spent years in places we'd hardly thought of. With them, we go to shops we'd never have entered, watch films we'd never have seen, hear about books and ideas that would never normally come our way. They spread their jam in an original manner; they give certain words a new intonation; their shoes come from a manufacturer we had never heard of. Their original sides lend us an opportunity to try out a different vision of existence.

The pleasures of secrecy

Being known is, at one level, our greatest longing. But being badly known is a prison. The phrase 'I know you' can be both a gift and a threatening way of asserting unwanted authority. Our partner claims to know us deeply, but in the process, they have often missed so much. An affair is a rebellion against this assumed, unfair knowledge. 'You don't know me at all' is the implicit message behind the raft of lies we are telling. They thought that they knew what was passing through our minds, but they have not the slightest clue about what is really happening in our lives right now. They may tell our friends what we are 'like', but they have no inkling of the itineraries we have devised to meet our lover in Rome, or what we have written to our passionate new companion in the app hidden on our phone. Our secret affair is a rebellion against the perils of being badly 'known'.

Revenge

We might not dare to put it this way, but there is a degree of delightful revenge in all this. Our partner assumed that no one else would care about us; they arrogantly believed that no one would look our way. They took our presence for granted. They couldn't bear to hear us to the end of our sentences. They disagreed with us relentlessly when they could so easily have given way. We are, through our lover, finding recompense for the many times when so much of what we cared for was trampled upon.

~

The majority position on affairs is, of course, that they are abhorrent. But they wouldn't be as widely practiced as they are were there not another side to the story that we don't typically dare to mention. It's by investigating the pleasures of affairs that we gain a sense of what can be so difficult about long-term love. Our affairs give us a measure of how much, how blindly and how badly we have hurt one another over the years.

THE PAINS OF AFFAIRS

We may think the problems of affairs are only too obvious, but they will probably surprise us all the same. It is worth attempting to look ahead at a few of them – not that they can (or even should) ever constitute a decisive argument against what we are planning.

Everyone is in tears

We begin with the hope that we can make ourselves happy, delight the lover and leave the long-term partner in pleasant ignorance. But as the story unfolds, the lover grows furious at our inability to commit, the partner is crushed by our betrayal and we are left in anxious, agonised tears at the chaos we have unleashed. There may be some children crying in the background as well, and if we are properly unlucky, moralistic neighbours or newspapers decrying our beastliness too. We cannot be blamed for our aspirations for contentment, but we can be roundly condemned for imagining that we could turn any of them into a sustainable reality.

We are denied a belief in our innocence

It seemed, at first, as if we had managed to escape the gravitational pull of our psychological weaknesses. We were no longer going to have to feel anxious, unconfident or ashamed. But soon enough we were reintroduced to our shadow sides, with an added disadvantage: We can no longer furiously blame the partner for preventing us from acceding to our better selves.

Blame is general

For a time, we had the satisfaction of knowing that the problem lay firmly with our partner; they were the ones holding us back, stifling our sex lives, hampering our ability to express ourselves professionally, dampening our mood and ruining our chances. But the affair has revealed a more awkward truth: that many of the greatest problems that hound us are endemic to us, or even to existence. We can see that we had previously experienced the pains of life in the company of our partner, not because of our partner.

The lover is human

We had to believe, in order to justify this adventure, that our lover did not partake of the ordinary mortal condition. We had to trust that they had not been touched by the stubborn errors and follies of regular humankind, that they would be free of the catalogue of sins we had noted over so many years in our partner's behaviour. But as the affair unfolded, we were inducted into a basic and sobering realisation: that the sins were not limited to our unfortunate spouse; the apparent angel could also at points grow tetchy, unreasonable, censorious, sharp-tongued and uninterested. We feel ready to accept a bitter truth: that love involves a process of exaggerating the difference between one person and another.

The dashed dreams of infidelity

So long as an affair remained only an abstract possibility, it could also be a source of comfort at moments of particular tension. We could, we told ourselves, if it were all to get too much, always have an affair. We knew it would not be easy, but it was an escape – and at points even a threat. But by turning that fantasy into a relationship, we have one less daydream to play with.

Guilt

This, naturally, is the greatest horror. In our bid for happiness, we have made others suffer. We have brought pain in our wake. We have engulfed those we love in sorrow. In more believing times, we could have fallen on our knees before a statue of a deity and begged for forgiveness. Now we must ask more haltingly for forgiveness from real people around us who are hurt and furious. There is no more transcendent cleansing available. We look in vain at the vast evening sky for deliverance. We thought ourselves kind and reasonable, but we have learnt that we were demented fools all along. We whisper idle sorries into our tear-stained pillows.

HOW TO REDUCE THE
RISK OF AFFAIRS

The traditional way to try to reduce the chances of someone having an affair is to focus on controlling their actions and outward movements: not letting them go to social events without us, calling them at random times or restricting their access to social media.

But people don't have affairs because they are able to meet attractive others; they have affairs because they feel emotionally disconnected from their partners. The best way to stop them from being tempted to sleep with someone else is not, therefore, to reduce their opportunities for contact; it is to leave them free to wander the world while ensuring that they feel heard by and reconciled with their partners. It is emotional closeness, not curfews, that guarantees the integrity of couples.

At a practical level, the route to closeness requires us to ensure that the two main sources of distance – resentment and loneliness – are correctly identified and regularly purged. The more we can tell our partners what we are annoyed and disappointed about, what we long for and are made by anxious by, and the more we can feel heard for doing so, the less we will bear grudges, take our distance and seek revenge by stripping naked with someone else. Few things are more properly Romantic (in the true sense of the word, meaning 'conducive to love') than highly honest conversations in which we have an opportunity to lay bare the particular ways in which our partners have disappointed us. Nothing may so endear us to someone as a chance to tell them why they have let us down.

To guide us in our restorative complaints, we might follow a range of questions and prompts:

I sometimes feel frustrated with you when ...

It sounds like a nasty theme, but handled correctly, it is the gateway to great tenderness and closeness. It provides us with an opportunity to do something very rare: level criticism without anger. And it's a chance to hear criticism as more than an attack, to interpret it for what it may truly be: a desire to learn how to live together with less occasion for anger.

I'd love you to realise that you hurt me when ...

We're carrying around wounds that we have, understandably and inevitably, found it hard to articulate. Perhaps the complaints sounded too petty or humiliating to mention at the time. The problem is that when they fester, the currents of affection start to get blocked, and soon we may find ourselves flinching when our partner tries to touch us. This prompt provides a safe moment in which to reveal a set of – typically entirely unintentional – hurts. Maybe last week there was something around work, or their mother, or the way they responded to a fairly innocent enquiry in the kitchen before a run. It's vital that the partner doesn't step in and deny that the hurt took place. There is no such thing as a hurt that is too small to matter when emotional closeness is at stake.

The hardest thing for you to understand about me is ...

We end up lonely because there is something important about who we are that the other appears not to grasp, and so – we can end up assuming – does not even want to take on board. But this lack of interest is rarely malevolent; it is usually more the case that there hasn't been a proper occasion for exploration. The feeling that one person knows another is the constant enemy of long-term couples. Our partners may understand us well, but we still need, patiently and diplomatically, to keep explaining things that remain unclear between us. We are changing all the time, we're no longer who we were last month and we can struggle to explain our own evolutions and needs even to ourselves. We must never be furious with our beloved for not grasping facets of our identity we haven't yet properly managed to share with them.

What I'd love you to appreciate about me is ...

We don't want untrammelled praise, but merely the odd moment when we can tell that what we feel is worthy of appreciation – maybe a little more appreciation than we have until now spontaneously received. We might want to draw attention to our best intentions (even when they didn't entirely work out), to the sweeter aspects of our character or to the good things about us which have quietly removed conflicts that would otherwise have emerged in the background. We're reminding ourselves and the other that there are reasons for us to deserve love.

Where I'm unfulfilled in my life is ...

It need not always be the fault of a lover that we are dissatisfied and restless. The longing for an affair can arise from a sense that the world more generally has not heard us, that we have been abandoned with career anxieties or that we are lagging behind our peers in terms of achievement and assets. Day to day, we tend not to explain the origins of these distressed moods very well. Our partner is the witness to them but can't easily recognise where the unhappiness is coming from. So they make the next most obvious move and start to assume that we are simply being mean or bad-tempered.

This prompt is a chance to explain the background existential fear and professional ennui responsible for some of our most acute day-to-day irritations and withdrawn states; a chance to demonstrate that we are not bad but are merely longing for their reassurance and support to battle our impression of insignificance and failure.

In order to be close to our partner and resist the lure of an affair, we also need to be able to speak with unusual candour about our sexual aspirations. Nothing more quickly reduces the need to act out a fantasy than the ability to speak about it and to be heard with sympathy, tolerance and curiosity. Here are some of the prompts that might induce the right sort of conversation about sex:

- *Something I'm really inhibited about sexually is ...*
- *I would love it if you could understand that sometimes I want ...*
- *What I wish I could change about me and sex is ...*
- *What I wish I could change about you and sex is ...*

No prompts can guarantee that an affair will never happen, but these could at least help to diagnose and repair the feelings of resentful distance or erotic loneliness that are the hidden drivers of the desire to wander off with someone else. We should dare to spend less time banning our partners from having lunch with strangers or travelling alone, and more time ensuring that they feel understood for their flaws and confusions – and appreciated for their virtues.

The idea that an affair could help a marriage sounds, naturally, rather paradoxical. Affairs are the enemies of marriages. They are what destroy established couples. There should be nothing positive whatsoever about one or both parties in a marriage heading off with a lover. And yet there are – perhaps strangely – a few ways in which an affair might contribute to the growth and stability of a union. In optimal situations, affairs deserve to be counted among the strange but genuine elements that can strengthen a marriage.

Here are a few of the reasons:

Liking ourselves more

Given how often we behave badly in love from feeling small and undesirable, a new person's interest can awaken us to a new sense of our own potency and sheer likeability, which we can take back into and use to nourish our primary relationship. Our romantic success can make us feel more able to cope with the irritants of ordinary life, helping us to recover the thread of our own self-esteem.

Guilt

We know a lot about how guilt can torment us; we know less about how it may motivate us to be kinder. Feeling that we have deeply wronged our partner can spur us to energetic attempts to recompense them for our deceit and mendacity. Rich in betrayal, we no longer stay fixated on their irritating habits and hurtful acts; we forget that they were unkind to us about our income or neglectful of our needs around the house. What we're chiefly aware of is that we told a panoply of appalling lies, lay with our lover in a bathtub while we texted our partner to say that a meeting had overrun, ignored the children on the weekends and wasted the household money on costly erotic gifts. And so we have, quite simply, no leg left to stand on. We may have to wait until we feel very bad indeed to start to do a bit of genuine good.

Practicing connection

We were driven into another's arms because we had forgotten the art of connection. We no longer knew how to be tender, give compliments, act playfully or behave with sensitivity and consideration. Our lover revised the emotional curriculum with us. In our hideaway, it became natural to touch them sweetly, to refer to them with an affectionate diminutive and to pick up on their best qualities. The affair was not just a school for betrayal; it turned out to be a school for love in its totality; its lessons could be transferred and reintegrated into the very relationship whose insufficiencies inspired the affair in the first place. In the process, the affair may start to seem a little less necessary. We can come to see that a lot of what we were seeking within the affair could, if only we remembered to practice certain moves, be available in the marriage.

Sex

We were desperate to re-experience ourselves as potent

and desirable. Our lover hasn't only helped us connect with them sexually; they've guided us back to our libido more broadly. It may be them in particular we made love to, but it's sex in general that they have given us an appetite for. We may not, at this point, always be thinking of our partner during sex. But we are, at least – much to their and our surprise – having sex with them once more.

Life is not elsewhere

Cheating lends us the gift of reducing the ill temper and angry wistfulness that can come from a sense that there must be beautiful, astonishing alternatives out there which our commitments have arbitrarily cut us off from. An affair puts our vagabond romantic imaginations usefully to the test; it challenges our unfair, sentimental suspicions that the pain and melancholy we sometimes feel is specifically the fault of our partner, rather than a general feature of existence. We may not always be happy with our long-term companion, but – the affair teaches us – nor would we invariably be happy with someone else either. That all relationships are complicated and, in certain ways, unsatisfying may be the wisest lesson that we can pull out of the burning, troubled embers of an affair.

No one is perfect

The affair teaches us that everyone is tricky from close up. Life with a new person would be differently, but equally, complex. It's a case of working out what variety of suffering we're best suited to. We stand to remember that we surrendered our freedom for very sound reasons, because we realised that we had found someone who was – in the end – about as good as any decent human can ever be expected to be. We are often unhappy, of course, but that is a universal law, not a unique curse.

We are not trapped

Instead of feeling that we have no option but to remain in our oppressive relationship, the affair gives us the opportunity fully to explore the idea that we could truly be with someone else. If, thereafter, we decide to stay in the marriage, the decision becomes once again a positive choice, not a habit or an arbitrary necessity. The conclusion that we want to remain functions like a renewal of vows. The best way to exorcise the power that affairs can have over married people is not to claim that they are both deeply lovely and yet entirely forbidden. It may be to give married people a chance to explore them and to see the reality from up close. As wise parents know, banning anything rarely works; it merely inflames our curiosity and arouses our defiance. The best move may be to give a restless partner a chance to find out what an affair is really like, and then have the nerve and wisdom to bet that the knowledge will return them to us soon enough.

Insofar as there could ever be a fruitful kind of cheating, it would be the sort that – without causing too much chaos or pain to all those involved – would quietly instruct us in one or two ways in which we could, once the affair is over, go on to have a slightly more successful and serene monogamous life.

WHAT IDEALLY HAPPENS WHEN
AN AFFAIR IS DISCOVERED?

What typically happens when an affair is discovered is fury on one side and a desperate show of contrition on the other. The person who has had the affair admits that they have done something evidently terrible for reasons that they are in no mood to defend. They were, they say meekly, merely being 'idiotic'. The partner, for their part, is deeply hurt and enraged – and encouraged to be even more so by most onlookers. They are shell-shocked by those lies about messages and meetings; they are struck by the monstrosity displayed by their spouse in undressing and having sex with someone else (when they were meant to be doing bath time). There are brutal accusations, tears and very long sulks. The relationship might be destroyed or it might continue, but there are sure to be high levels of hostility and distrust long into the future. The guilty partner will know that they can never now make any legitimate complaints, nor expect any mercy or tenderness. Their task will be to atone, more or less without end.

But there's another possibility which can be sketched out, initially in its fantasy form. In this case, when the affair is discovered, the key factor won't be seen as the sex or the hotel meetings or the kisses in the bathroom. Rather, the affair will be understood as a symptom of an unhappiness that both partners can be committed to exploring and resolving without rancour: the real issue will firmly be 'what led to the affair?' not 'how dare you.'

The focus will be on how it came about that one of them got into an affair-ready state. The discussion won't be powered by jealousy but by open-minded curiosity. The real target of investigation won't be when the meetings took place or what happened in the seaside B&B; it will be the task of uncovering the moments of emotional disconnection that unfolded during the long years before the fateful tryst.

Together the couple might go through how they came to take one another for granted, how one of them felt misunderstood or abandoned or ignored, why it was so difficult to address their hurt and how things might be set right in the future. The burden wouldn't be placed solely on the shoulders of the one who had the affair. It would be accepted, with immense maturity, that there must have been problems on both sides. The one who, in normal terms, was 'betrayed' would concede that the liaison was only partly the unfaithful partner's responsibility. For their part, the one who had the affair wouldn't focus overly on their own guilt; they would be concerned about and saddened by their inability, at a sufficiently early stage, properly to communicate their growing distress and alienation. They would locate their error not around having had sex with someone else but around failing to work out how to communicate their emotional wounds properly and in good time to their partner.

Instead of being destroyed, the relationship would thereby be improved, because the couple would emerge with a much better understanding of how to avoid the kind of emotional disconnection that inspired the affair in the first place. Looking back on their relationship, they would identify the affair as an important turning point after which they gradually learnt to be more patient, more understanding and more communicative partners to one another.

Admittedly, this is an ideal. Few of us will manage such exemplary behaviour. There are likely to be irrational scenes. But the hope is that, despite the anger and the sense of betrayal, there can truly at some stage be a recognition that the affair didn't happen by accident or from nowhere. It will be viewed as something evidently bad but also poignantly comprehensible; one person may be much more guilty, but it can't be that the other had no role at all in creating an affair-ready state. And an affair won't be seen as a symptom of a mean-minded desire to exit the relationship so much as a dangerously distorted plea for intimacy and connection – an attempt, however wrongly enacted, by one person to communicate to another what they so desperately wanted and needed from love.

HOW TO HANDLE THE
DESIRE FOR AFFAIRS

In a better world, affairs wouldn't continuously threaten those with monogamous aspirations. Couples would quickly recognise when emotional disconnection was building up between them and they would take direct, timely steps to articulate their hurts and so avoid ever slipping into an affair-ready state. Or, if infidelity did occur, the sexual dimension would be interpreted first and foremost as a symptom of emotional distance, which would then be corrected through candid discussion.

Couples wouldn't be tormented by fear and guilt on the one hand, and anger and a sense of betrayal on the other.

But there are entrenched features of human nature and of our social arrangements that work powerfully against this utopian vision. Moments of emotional disconnection are, to a greater or lesser extent, almost inevitable and often unfold without our being entirely aware of them. We don't tend to realise early enough the degree to which we are upsetting one another, and fail to acknowledge even to ourselves how distressed we have grown. Furthermore, we lack a native talent for explaining our resentments or for the focused calm required to work through our troubles in the flux of daily life.

The desire for an affair will, therefore, never entirely or

spontaneously disappear. So what options do we possess for at least attenuating it? A number of moves, habits of mind and practices suggest themselves:

Relationship therapy

Long-term relationships are impossible to imagine without areas of friction and disappointment; there will be misunderstandings and miscommunications; there will be varying levels of resentment on both sides. In response, our modern Romantic culture tends to suggest that we should spend more time together and 'talk more'. It assumes that the healing of problems can be a spontaneous and instinctive process, that all we need to do is to create more opportunities for quiet dinners or country walks. It's a pleasing idea, but one that, in reality, is unlikely to work. Once a sufficient degree of resentment has built up, it grows harder for two people to accurately and effectively discuss their troubles. They're more likely to flare up or get hurt, or fall into sullen silence and vicious circles of accusation.

Relationship therapy operates with a very different view. It assumes from the start that constructive communication around resentment is enormously difficult and that we therefore require a lot of structure and guidance if we're ever successfully going to unpick what's bothering us. We're going to need the presence of a third party who has spent years studying what can go badly or well around communication. They will need to ask questions in a systematic way to discover the true sources of our suppressed rage; they will have to listen for what's not being directly said but only hinted at; they will have to extract an important essence from a lot of exaggerated or angry remarks; they will need to remain unpanicked by their clients' conflicts because they have encountered such things so many times before. They will take the conversation into less expected but more helpful places, discussing moments that may have happened long before the couple met but which have continued to shape their engagement.

The goal of therapy is not a perfect relationship; it is to make some level of disconnection bearable to both parties. It is to reduce resentment and move the couple away from an affair-ready state. It is to advance a notion that a relationship can be good enough even though it is not precisely what either person would, in fantasy, have liked it to be.

Relationship therapy looks like something that we could be interested in only when a relationship is failing; in fact, it may be the single greatest tool that can help to prevent it from doing so.

Erotic friendship

Romantic culture demands that our partner be everything to us; a far kinder approach is to recognise that friends should be allowed to supplement our partner, without this being viewed as a sin or a betrayal.

At some point we might meet another person with whom we feel a lot of sexual sympathy. Maybe at a party they say something about their desires that clicks with us; they laugh in a lovely, responsive way when a particular erotic topic is touched on in a general discussion. We sense from their tone of voice, from the way they dress or move, from little things they say that they would understand us erotically to a precise degree.

There might, in such circumstances, be no question at all of having an actual affair. We may not wish to endanger our primary relationship in any way. However, when we spend time with this friend, we may feel that our sexuality is understood and liked. They are fascinated when we tell them about the stranger recesses of our desires; they let us into their more secret passions. We discuss longings and difficulties and hang-ups and things we find intriguing or exciting. We have a consoling and entertaining time with them and experience a marked reduction in our feelings of shame.

We're not lovers, just friends, but by talking to them, we end up critically reassured: things we thought were very odd about ourselves are, in their eyes, revealed as beguiling and interesting. Parts of ourselves that felt lonely discover a longed-for companion.

Finding another person who is interested in meeting us

in this way takes a crucial amount of pressure off our main relationship. We don't have to look to our long-term partner for everything. We can accept a little more graciously the fact that, at points, they are bored or put off by some of our thoughts.

And because there's no sex – and no plan for sex – this kind of friendship can be accepted with grace by our long-term partner. One of the best guarantees of long-term love is not to insist that our partner be everything whatsoever for us.

A better kind of prostitution

Prostitution is a natural target for immense hostility, in part because modern sensibilities are so upset by the idea of physical sex occurring outside of stable, loving relationships.

But we can imagine a revised form of prostitution that would have a very different focus. The service provided by this utopian version would be much more like a kind of erotic friendship than a sexual outlet. We would be accessing a skilled professional who offered not intercourse but affection and understanding. For a fee, we would pass an hour or two with someone adept at making us feel liked and heard; they would give us warm and well-judged compliments; they would tease out the complex workings of our sexual imaginations; they would make us feel acceptable and desirable, and send us back out into the world better able to negotiate the tensions of ordinary relationships. Physical sex would not need to be anywhere on the agenda. But these revised brothels would be meeting the very psychological needs that often drive people into destructive and ill-judged affairs.

A central source of inspiration would come from the Japanese tradition of the geisha. In medieval Japan, geishas were available for hire but didn't offer a directly sexual service. Instead they were concerned with gifting visitors a more general erotic connection. Geishas might be playful and teasing, they might make suggestive remarks or create an atmosphere of acceptance and sympathy. But there was understood to be no need for sex itself.

The figure of the geisha might have been connected to very specific features of Japanese culture, but the underlying idea they bear is universal. At its most objective, prostitution could be described as a service targeting erotic demands that are not met within marriage or long-term relationships. We are still at the dawn of discovering what such a service might really be in its dignified form and how much it might help couples without either humiliating its providers or degrading its users.

Masturbation

Masturbation is founded upon a crucial philosophical distinction between imagination and action. There are many things it is exciting to think about that it would be far from a good idea actually to initiate. We readily recognise this around novels. We might love reading a story set in St Petersburg in 1918, though we'd viscerally hate to have had to live through the chaos and violence of the Russian Revolution.

Equally, we can enjoy imagining having sex with someone we recently met through our work or at a garden party with friends, even though we recognise immediately that, in reality, the act would be a disaster.

Imagination carefully edits out very real difficulties. In the literary imagination we can join a character in prison – we can hear the sound of the guard's footsteps outside and the shouts of someone being interrogated in the next cell – while we ourselves are comfortably lying on a sofa, working through a bowl of pistachio nuts.

Likewise, in the privacy of our own heads, we can write central sections of an erotic novel of an affair without having to set in motion anything in reality, and without all the awkward and distressing emotions this would surely entail.

It is one of the wonders of the human constitution, and one that lies at the heart of our masturbatory talents, that we are far from needing to do everything that it can be so pleasant to think about. Whatever can be beautifully dreamt of no longer so urgently needs to be acted out.

Secrets far away

Romanticism equates love with total honesty. But this sets up in our minds – and in our collective culture – a powerful and potentially very problematic ideal: the notion that if two people properly love one another, they must always tell each other the truth about everything.

Yet over the long term there are always things we may do that have a power to hurt and deeply offend those we love. This brings us up against a fundamental paradox within the modern understanding of love: Keeping secrets seems like a betrayal of a relationship, but the complete truth can, if shared, place a union in mortal danger.

We are perhaps so conscious of the bad reasons for hiding things that we haven't paid enough attention to the noble reasons why, from time to time, true loyalty may lead one to say very much less than the whole truth. We are so impressed by honesty that we forget the virtues of selective secrecy, which doesn't have to mean a cynical withholding of important information, but a dedication to not rubbing someone up against the full and more hurtful aspects of one's nature.

What makes falsehoods at points necessary is our proclivity for making unfortunate associations. It is, in theory, of course entirely possible to love someone deeply and at the same time to spend a night with someone else. But in every betrayed person's mind, the tryst becomes synonymous with the rejection of their entire being. This forces any half-decent person to lie. It is because the betrayed person is in the grip of what is in essence a falsehood ('If you express any sexual interest in someone else, you can't like me') that one has to offer a dose of untruth ('I went to bed early'), by which we can make sure that a big truth ('I love you deeply') remains safe.

Suppose a married person goes away to a conference. One night, after a lovely conversation in the bar, she gets carried away and slips into bed with an international colleague. They rub their lips together and entwine their legs. They will almost certainly never see one another again, it wasn't an attempt to start a long-term relationship and it meant very little. When the woman gets home, her partner asks how her evening was. She says she watched CNN and ordered a club sandwich in her room on her own.

She lies because she knows her partner well and can predict how he would respond to the truth. He would be wounded to the core, would be convinced that his wife didn't love him and would conclude that divorce was the only option. But this assessment of the truth would not be true. In reality, it is of course possible to love someone deeply and every so often to go to bed with another person. And yet, kind people understand the entrenched and socially endorsed associations between infidelity and callousness. For almost all of us, the news 'I spent a night with a colleague from the Singapore office' (which is true) has to end up meaning 'I don't love you anymore' (which is not true at all). And so we have to say, 'I didn't sleep with anyone' (which is untrue), in the name of securing the greater idea, 'I still love you' (which is overwhelmingly true).

However much they love the truth, good people have an even greater commitment to something else: being kind towards others. They grasp (and make allowances for) the ease with which a truth can produce desperately unhelpful convictions in the minds of others and are therefore not proudly over-committed to accuracy at every turn. Their loyalty is reserved for something they take to be far more important than literal narration: the sanity and well-being of their audiences. Telling the truth, they understand, isn't a matter of the sentence-by-sentence veracity of one's words; it's a matter of ensuring that, after one has spoken, the other person can be left with a true picture of reality.

It is ultimately no great sign of kindness to insist on showing someone our entire selves at all times. Repression, a certain degree of restraint and a dedication to editing one's pronouncements belong to love as much as a capacity for explicit confession. The person who cannot tolerate secrets, who in the name of 'being honest' always has to share information so wounding it cannot be forgotten, is no friend of love.

Furthermore, if we suspect (and we should, rather regularly, if the relationship is a good one) that our partner might be lying a bit too (about what they are thinking about, about who they are messaging or about where they were last night), it is perhaps best not to lay into them like a sharp inquisitor, however intensely we might yearn to do just that. It may be kinder, wiser and perhaps more in the true spirit of love to pretend we simply haven't noticed anything.

The fetish of cuckoldry

Being a cuckold – the husband of an adulterous wife – is traditionally viewed as one of the most degraded of all situations. However, in recent times, cuckoldry has more interestingly emerged as a powerful sexual fetish, celebrated in pornography and promoted in clubs and societies. In certain couples, males (and also females) are invited to witness their partner's sexual excitement at the hands of somebody else, and far from this being framed as a betrayal, it is enjoyed as an act that reminds one partner of the value and appeal of their companion, in a way that will help the couple themselves to reconnect with their own erotic powers.

The demand that our partner can't ever have sex with anyone else may appear to be a sign of closeness, but – ironically – it can function as a remarkably punitive, even cruel injunction that may produce pervasive feelings of oppression and resentment. Our sense of ownership over the other diminishes their self-confidence in their eyes and their allure and value in our own.

The operative principle within sexualised cuckoldry can be observed in many other areas of life, for example, home ownership. We might have grown rather bored of where we live. We may chiefly be preoccupied by poor ventilation in the bedroom, by a shower door that doesn't close properly and by some unfortunate marks on the hallway wall. But when a friend comes around and is openly appreciative of the view from the sitting room window and of the elegant layout of the downstairs rooms, we realise, thanks to their enthusiasm, how much there is to value about where we live. Similarly, the sexual interest of a third person can reignite our capacity to admire our partner when we are alone. Far from humiliating us, the newcomer is doing us the immense favour of reminding us of why we devoted ourselves to our spouse in the first place.

Cuckoldry is an extreme-sounding but, in fact, possibly sensible attempt to do something important: reacquaint ourselves with the idea of our partner as a free and independent individual capable of generating desire in many people – and to do so in an atmosphere of trust and openness.

When our partner is excited by another person, we're very dramatically reminded that they don't belong to us and they have a power – which should ultimately flatter us as well – over others. These facts are normally encountered only with considerable horror when an affair is uncovered. But they might be introduced more gently, and with far greater erotic and psychological benefit, when all parties subscribe openly to a fetishistic game of cuckoldry. The potential cruelty of an affair for the 'betrayed' one can thereby be turned into joy at witnessing how much delight a stranger can derive from undressing a lover they had for too long forgotten how to desire.

WHAT DOES IT TAKE TO
BE GOOD AT AFFAIRS?

Affairs are not for everyone. Though we might imagine that all of us might one day be embroiled in one through impulse, they require a set of skills that not all of us possess.

It is by asking ourselves what we might need to be good at in order to succeed at affairs (and by implication why we might fail dismally at them), that we stand to gain important knowledge of what powers and guides infidelity and who among us would best be advised to give affairs a go:

The art of feeling misunderstood

A fundamental prerequisite for being good at affairs is a mastery of the art of feeling misunderstood: a proclivity for believing that our partner has failed to appreciate important things about us and that the hurt could never be set right through generous and in-depth conversations. The skilled adulterer must additionally be a master of the neighbouring art of believing that 'the other should have known', that the partner who has apparently let them down should more readily have understood them (perhaps without them even needing to speak) and has reneged on an implicit duty to provide them with constant consolation and well-being. Good adulterers need to be, in their primary relationships, in their own way, very idealistic.

The marriages of others

Good adulterers know that other couples are not suffering quite so badly. Not for most marriages the strained conversations, the boring evenings and the fractious family holidays they know so well from their own lives. Other people are having fun – their behaviour at dinner promises as much. Other spouses are kinder and more inclined to want sex; they don't argue in the car or sulk through the bank holiday weekend. It is evident that a special curse, which stands to be corrected, has been visited on them.

Compartmentalisation

Affairs require an advanced ability to handle diverging moods and emotional atmospheres. One minute we are caressing our lover's backside and experimenting with a sexual implement; the next we are outside the school gates, waiting to ask our child how geography went this afternoon. We need to be able to sit through dinner with our in-laws and have the confidence that none of our thoughts are leaking out of our heads or are legible on our brows. We need mental strongboxes and bunkers.

Deception

Good adulterers have to know how to keep an unflinching and resolute face while spinning an entirely fantastical account of what they were up to on the weekend in Argentina or at the conference in Hanoi. They have to be able to find an immediate answer to the question of who they were typing to just now on the phone. They may have only minutes to explain who they were with in a fish restaurant downtown at lunchtime. It helps in all this if we can, albeit only momentarily, actually believe the lie that we are telling, if we can untether ourselves from the normal tyranny of facts and properly identify with the phantasm we have woven. To be convincing, we need to imagine with particular clarity that it really was an aunt we were with in the restaurant and that our phone really did run out of battery on the weekend. Adulterers momentarily know that they really do have a dog and that it really did eat the homework.

Self-justification

The good adulterer knows how to keep the score and how to remind themselves why – though this is obviously not very nice – the affair is not at all unwarranted either. They are, in the end, allowed to do this because the other ruined the holiday last year, because they rarely listen, because they seldom initiate, because they were short-tempered when the children were small, because they have often refused to listen to their views on politics and once threw away a favourite book or coat of theirs. Successful adulterers have learnt the art of feeling innocent and compassionate for themselves, and of not letting empathy or alternative perspectives get in the way of their plans for comeuppance.

Steady nerves

The partner's reaction can never be entirely predicted. There might be a sudden call to the lawyers, nosey neighbours, the involvement of social media, a ruinous divorce, gossip at work or damage that spreads to the children. The adulterous have heard all the risks. They also know that the ice caps might melt and nuclear warheads may fall into the hands of terrorists. But they are robust enough to concentrate on what generally happens, not on what could occur in extremis. They hear the police siren in the street outside as they lie exhausted after coitus next to their lover and don't worry that it might be on its way to see them.

Boredom

Affairs are, if nothing else, profoundly exciting. They will, therefore, be of particular appeal to the bored, to people whose working lives feel very routine, who are beset by a sense of staleness and who aren't deriving any significant pleasure from friends, travel, art or their own minds. Affairs are of particular interest to those who lack imagination.

Pre-Romantics

Romanticism was a movement in the arts that spread rapidly and overwhelmingly through European and then global civilisation in the period after 1750. But there still remain a few redoubts that battle its philosophy, a few strongholds against the belief that good marriages have to involve exclusive degrees of love and sexual interest, a few places where an older aristocratic mindset still reigns and allows for an unanguished separation between one's duties to the family on the one hand and one's commitment to erotic pleasure on the other. Here and there, in apartments in the Ile de France or villas in the plains of Lombardy, it is possible to leave a dinner with one's spouse and children and, without compunction, take a scooter to the other side of town to rejoin one's lover in a rented apartment. One is thereby following tradition no less dutifully than if one took up an honorary mayoral post or honoured the community with a gift at harvest time.

Those counting the days

People particularly aware of their own impending physical decline may grow powerfully less concerned with the consequences of their actions on the lives of others. Death strengthens the soul against the pull of excessive guilt and compassion. Panicked by the ticking of the clock, the mortally aware grab their pleasures where they still can. Death renders them more courageous about pushing themselves forward. They will ask for the phone number and suggest lunch or the trip to Vienna. They are especially sensitive to the nubility of flesh and the fall and cut of garments. They can be haunted by the sight of a small tattoo or a nose ring and remain infinitely generous towards immaturities of mind where these coexist with a grace of form. They are too worried and too sad to leave this particular kind of pleasure alone; they need to embrace it with manic energy as a defence against the terrors of disintegration and the onset of night.

~

Some of us are in no way ideologically opposed to affairs. The idea may appeal hugely. And yet, in the course of pursuing them, we may discover that we have no real stomach for what they entail. We may find out – while unexpectedly unnerved at the start of a lie, or visited by guilty nausea in the playground – that we lack the temperament for them, that affairs are a skill and that, much to our regret and that of our fledgling lover, we may simply lack the talent to pull them off successfully.

AFFAIRS AND HIGH HORSES

Whatever its benefits and pains, being involved in an affair should, if nothing else, once and for all, cure us of any tendency to moralise – that is, to look harshly and with strict judgement on the misdemeanours and follies of others.

An affair should naturally induct us into the full scale of our mendacity, impatience, weakness, cowardliness, derangement and sentimentality. We should thereafter never be able to feel impervious and superior when hearing of certain insane things that others have done in the name of love or desire. We will have joined the legions of the sexually chastened, who can have no more illusions as to their own purity or steadiness of mind. We won't be able to feel that only monsters are led by the body or sacrifice everything for passion.

And yet we won't be able to give up on ourselves entirely either; we'll have to keep going with life and somehow find a way to forgive ourselves for the days and nights we lost to our madness. At best, we will learn how to laugh darkly at ourselves, to know at all times that – however grand and authoritative some parts of our lives might seem – we are only ever millimetres away from tragedy and lunacy.

Our affairs will force us to dismount from our high horses and forever do away with any sense of superiority, to graciously accept that we are complete idiots now –

always have been and always will be. From there we will have no option but to go on to be infinitely kind and unendingly generous towards anyone who ever wants to have, or has ever been involved in, those delightful, wretched, tumultuous, destructive and utterly compelling adventures we call affairs.

THE LOVE SERIES

There is no more joyful or troublesome area of our lives than love. From adolescence onwards, it is rare to go for any sustained length of time without some sort of fascinating or devilish new problem emerging around relationships.

The Love Series by The School of Life aims to be like an ideal friend around the dilemmas of the heart. Each title zeroes in on one of the central issues we're liable to confront – from dating to heartbreak, from affairs to arguments. What unites the books is their combination of psychological insight, humanity and warmth: they lend us the advice and comfort we need to find the happiness we deserve.